TRUE OR FALSE?

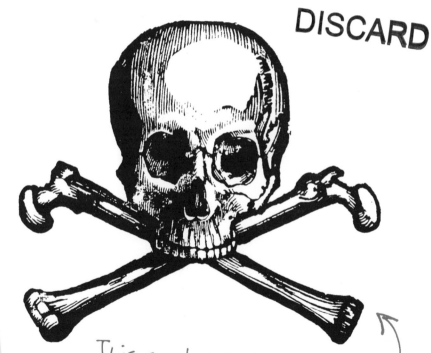

This symbol is the logo for a famous theme park. It welcomes millions of visitors each year.

FALSE!

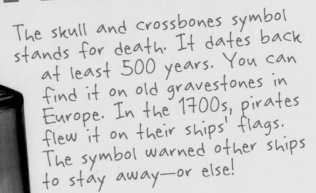

The skull and crossbones symbol stands for death. It dates back at least 500 years. You can find it on old gravestones in Europe. In the 1700s, pirates flew it on their ships' flags. The symbol warned other ships to stay away—or else!

Since the 1850s, the symbol has been used to label dangerous poisons. Check out this bottle. It's like ones made in the 1800s. Poisonous liquids were often stored in these glass containers. The skull sign warned people to handle with care.

Book design: Red Herring Design/NYC

Library of Congress Cataloging-in-Publication Data
Prokos, Anna.
Killer wallpaper : true cases of deadly poisonings / by Anna Prokos.
p. cm. — (24/7 : science behind the scenes)
Includes bibliographical references and index.
ISBN-13: 978-0-531-12061-3 (lib. bdg.)   978-0-531-15459-5 (pbk.)
ISBN-10: 0-531-12061-9 (lib. bdg.)   0-531-15459-9 (pbk.)
1. Poisons—Juvenile literature. 2. Toxicology—Juvenile literature.
I. Title.
RA1213.P76 2007
615.9—dc22   2006005873

FRANKLIN WATTS and associated logos are trademarks and/or registered
trademarks of Scholastic Library Publishing. SCHOLASTIC and associated logos
are trademarks and/or registered trademarks of Scholastic Inc.
1 2 3 4 5 6 7 8 9 10 R 16 15 14 13 12 11 10 09 08 07

KILLER WALLPAPER

True Cases of Deadly Poisonings

Anna Prokos

WARNING: This book is highly toxic! It contains poison, drugs, and deadly chemicals—in places you'd least expect! What's on these pages can kill you! Consider this your final warning . . .

Franklin Watts®
A Division of Scholastic Inc.
New York • Toronto • London • Auckland • Sydney
Mexico City • New Delhi • Hong Kong
Danbury, Connecticut

CONTENTS

Get a spoonful of information about what forensic toxicologists really do.

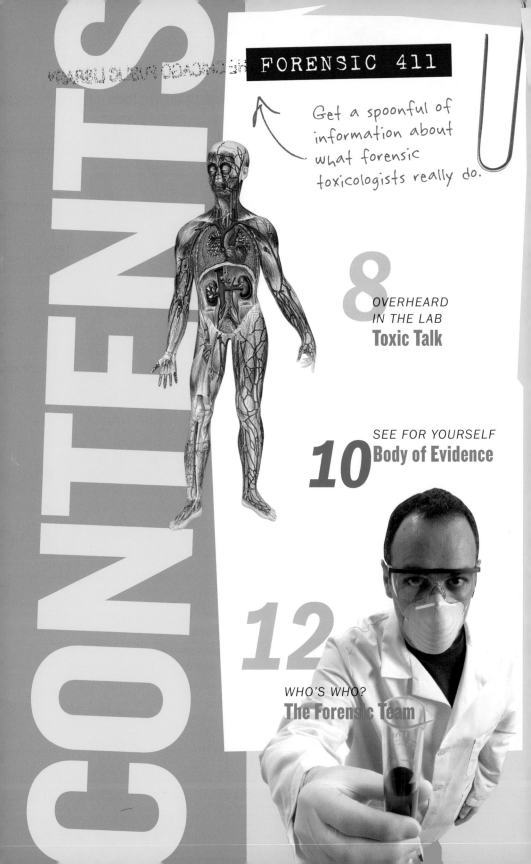

TRUE-LIFE CASE FILES!

These cases are 100% real. Find out how toxicologists helped solve some poisonous mysteries.

Someone in Washington put poison in this pain killer.

15 Case #1:
The Case of the Deadly Drug
Two people are dead after taking a common pain medicine. Who could have poisoned the pills?

25 Case #2:
The Case of the Poisoned Politician
One night, Viktor Yushchenko is battling for the presidency of Ukraine. The next day, he is fighting for his life.

Was a presidential candidate in Ukraine poisoned?

The emperor may have died from arsenic poisoning.

35 Case #3:
The Case of the Royal Poisoning
French Emperor Napoleon Bonaparte dies after a strange illness. Can a lock of hair solve this historical mystery?

FORENSIC DOWNLOAD

Here's even more amazing stuff about forensic toxicology for you to swallow.

100 GMS.
Ether, Squibb
FOR ANÆSTHESIA

E·R·SQUIBB & SONS
MANUFACTURING CHEMISTS TO THE MEDICAL PROFESSION SINCE 1858
NEW YORK

YELLOW PAGES

A body is found. It shows no signs of violence. Police can't find fingerprints or a murder weapon. What happened?

FORENSIC 411

The victim may have been poisoned. If so, the body still holds traces of the poison. What was it? Where did it come from? Finding out is a job for a forensic toxicologist.

Toxic Talk

toxicology
(TOK-sik-ahl-uh-jee) the science of finding, treating, and studying poisons. Toxicologists study how poisons affect plants, animals, the environment, and humans.

"There's no obvious cause of death. Make sure you get **toxicology** results on the body."

"Toxic" has to do with poison. "Ology" means "the study of."

"Did the victim have any strange **symptoms** before she passed out?"

symptoms
(SIMP-tums) signs of an illness or some physical problem

"I'm starting to suspect that she might have been accidentally **poisoned**."

poisoned
(POY-zuhnd) taken a substance that causes injury, illness, or death

8

"Test for every drug you can think of. She took something toxic, and I want to know what it was."

drug
(druhg) a product or chemical that can change the way the body works. Drugs from a doctor can be used to treat illnesses.

toxic
(TOK-sik) poisonous

"This might not be murder. They found deadly toxins in a waste dump not far from here."

toxin
(TOK-sihn) any substance that can kill cells or cause injury or death; a poison

Say What?

Here's some other lingo a forensic toxicologist might use on the job.

acute
(uh-KYOOT) describing a poisoning that is quick and intense
"The victim was fine yesterday. This must be a case of acute poisoning."

chain of custody
(chayn uhv KUH-stuh-dee) the list of people who handle evidence, in the order in which they handle it. In court, lawyers can attack toxicology tests if evidence is not handled properly.
"This is an important case. Make sure there are no mistakes on the chain of custody for the blood sample."

chronic
(KRAH-nik) describing a poisoning that happens over time in small doses
"This was a case of chronic poisoning. The victim had symptoms for months before she died."

HAIR: In a living person, hair stores toxins much longer than blood or urine. That helps **forensic** toxicologists test for drugs and other toxins.

STOMACH, INTESTINES, LIVER: Gulp! Any drug that's been swallowed travels from the stomach to the intestines and the liver.

LUNGS: If a toxin is in gas form, it will probably leave traces in a **victim**'s lungs.

STOMACH: Toxicologists look at the stomach to find out how much of a drug was digested before death. The results can help them figure out when a drug was taken.

BLOOD: Blood is a toxicologist's best friend. Nearly every drug can be found in the blood. Blood tests can show how much of a toxin was taken and how it affected the body.

KIDNEYS: Kidneys filter waste—including poisons—out of the blood. They turn the waste into urine so the body can get rid of it. Toxicologists test urine for toxins.

MUSCLES: Some drugs enter the body through a needle. Those drugs may go directly into a muscle. Toxicologists test muscles around the needle mark to find out what kind of drug is present.

EYES: The liquid in your eyeballs is called *vitreous humor*. Many **chemicals** found in the blood end up here. It takes about two hours for a poison to travel from your blood to your vitreous humor. Testing the liquid can help determine the time of death.

Body of Evidence

Poisons end up in different places in the human body. Here's where toxicologists look for signs of poisoning.

LIVER: The liver filters toxins from the blood. Then it turns the toxins into a liquid called bile. Testing the liver and the **bile** can show when a poison was taken. It can tell toxicologists if a poisoning was acute or chronic.

INSECTS: Insects that feed off of a dead body take in chemicals from the person's body. Toxicologists sometimes test these bugs to look for **evidence** of drugs in a victim.

TISSUES: Drugs that are injected with a needle may not show up in the stomach or liver. They can often be found in tissues almost anywhere else in the body.

11

The Forensic Team

Forensic toxicologists work as part of a team. Here's a look at some of the experts who help solve crimes.

FORENSIC ENTOMOLOGISTS

They study the insects on or near a body. They can also figure out if there are poisons in bugs found on the victim's body.

FIRST RESPONDER POLICE OFFICERS/ DETECTIVES

They are often the ones to find, collect, and transport the evidence. They take photos and give the forensic toxicologist the crime scene data.

FORENSIC PATHOLOGISTS/ MEDICAL EXAMINERS

They're medical doctors who investigate suspicious deaths. They try to find out when and how someone died. They often direct other members of the team.

FORENSIC TOXICOLOGISTS

They test victims for drugs, alcohol, and/ or poison.

FORENSIC ANTHROPOLOGISTS

They're called in to identify victims by studying bones.

LAWYERS

They argue cases in court. They either defend someone accused of a crime, or they try to prove that the suspect is guilty.

FINGERPRINT EXAMINERS

They find, photograph, and collect fingerprints at the scene. Then they compare them to prints they have on record.

FORENSIC DENTISTS

They identify victims and criminals by their teeth or bitemarks.

TRUE-LIFE CASE FILES!

24 hours a day, 7 days a week, 365 days a year, forensic toxicologists are solving mysteries.

IN THIS SECTION:

▶ how a few strange green specks helped FBI AGENTS put a poisoner in jail;

▶ whether a presidential candidate was REALLY POISONED;

▶ why TOXICOLOGISTS think a famous emperor may not have died of natural causes.

Here's how forensic toxicologists get the job done.

What does it take to solve a crime? Good forensic toxicologists don't just make guesses. They're scientists. They follow a step-by-step process.

As you read the case studies, you can follow along with these scientists. Keep an eye out for the icons below. They'll clue you in to each step along the way.

 At the beginning of a case, toxicologists **identify one or two main questions** they have to answer.

 The next step is to **gather and analyze evidence**. Toxicologists collect blood or tissue samples. They gather as much evidence as they can. Then they test it to see what they can conclude.

 Finally, toxicologists **study the test results to reach a conclusion**. If they've done their job well, their evidence might help crack the case.

Auburn, Washington
June 11, 1986
6:43 A.M.

The Case of the Deadly Drug

**Two people are dead after taking
a common pain medicine. Who could
have poisoned the pills?**

"Something's Wrong with Her!"

**A healthy mom drops dead in the bathroom.
What could have killed her?**

After she collapsed, Sue Snow was rushed by helicopter to Harborview Medical Center in Seattle. But it was too late.

The 911 call came at 6:43 A.M. on June 11, 1986. Fifteen-year-old Hayley Snow had trouble getting the words out. "I think my mother fell while I was in the shower.... She's breathing and everything, but something's wrong with her."

In the bathroom at their home in Auburn, Washington, Sue Snow lay on the floor. Her eyes were open, staring at the wall. Yet she didn't seem to be **conscious**. She couldn't talk to Hayley, and she was gasping for air.

Emergency medical technicians arrived while Hayley was still on the phone. Sue Snow was taken by helicopter to Harborview Medical Center in Seattle. She died there several hours later.

Doctors at Harborview couldn't explain what happened. At 40, Sue Snow was in perfect health. How could she have died so suddenly?

What's going on in Auburn, Washington? On June 11, 1986, a healthy 40-year-old collapsed in this suburb of Seattle. Another death was reported across town. Did they both die of natural causes? Or was there a killer on the loose?

The Scent of Almonds

**It's time for an autopsy and drug tests.
Was Sue Snow poisoned?**

On the day Sue Snow died, the police collected all the pills from her home. This is just one of the pills that was collected as evidence and sent for testing.

Doctors ordered an **autopsy** for Sue Snow. Dr. Corinne Fligner, the assistant **ME**, or medical examiner, went to work. Her assistant, Janet Miller, made the first incision. A faint but clear scent rose from the body: almonds. Miller knew right away what it was. "I smell **cyanide**," she told Fligner.

It turned out that Miller was right. Fligner sent a sample of Snow's blood to the toxicology lab. On June 16, the tests came back positive. Most likely, Snow had been murdered.

The case began to sound familiar to police. In 1982, a killer in the Chicago area secretly slipped cyanide into Tylenol capsules. Seven people died after taking the poisoned pills. According to Snow's daughter, Snow had taken two Excedrin pain relievers half an hour before she died. Was it possible that a copycat killer was poisoning Excedrin capsules?

Just after lunch, police officers arrived at Sue Snow's house. Her husband agreed to allow a search. Police took every pill bottle they could find, including an opened bottle of Excedrin. They sent the pills to a lab for testing.

Just after 8 P.M., the results came in. Nine of the 56 capsules had cyanide in them.

A KILLER POISON
How cyanide does its dirty work.

Anyone who's read detective novels knows about cyanide. As a powder, it has very little smell or taste. A tiny pinch can be fatal. It can kill in minutes.

Despite how deadly it is, cyanide isn't hard to buy. Photographers use it to develop film. Jewelry makers use it in metalworking. It's found in insect poisons and blue dyes. You can even find it in certain foods. Apricot pits, almonds, lima beans, and spinach have cyanide in them. But the amounts are small enough to be harmless.

Doctors find the symptoms hard to identify. The one sign is a faint smell of bitter almonds that only some people can smell.

Cyanide put Sue Snow in a **coma** in less than an hour. It kills by making cells unable to use oxygen. It left Snow gasping for air to get more oxygen into her body.

Killer on the Loose
The FBI takes over—and the body count goes up to two.

On June 17, the **FBI** took over Sue Snow's murder case. Special Agent Jack Cusack was ordered to lead the investigation. By now, the death was big news. Drug companies offered a reward for information about the killer.

Dozens of FBI agents went to drugstores in the Seattle area. They collected thousands of Excedrin bottles. Right away, tests found a second poisoned bottle.

Bristol-Myers is the company that made Excedrin. Executives there ordered stores around the country to take all the bottles off their shelves.

That day, a strange call led local police to bottles three and four. The caller was a 42-year-old woman named Stella Nickell.

Nickell told police that her husband, Bruce, had died 12 days earlier. The ME had said that the cause was lung disease. But Stella Nickell told police that her husband had taken four Excedrin just before he died. She thought he must have been poisoned. She had even called the ME's office three times to question their decision.

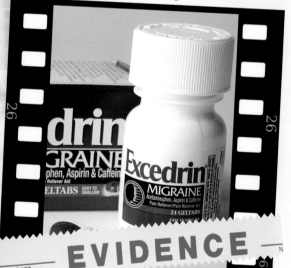

Nickell handed over two Excedrin bottles. She had bought them at two different stores. In two days, the test results were in. Between the bottles, six pills contained cyanide.

On June 24, agents found a fifth poisoned bottle in a local drugstore.

The police collected all the Excedrin from Stella Nickell's house. Had her husband also died from poisoned pills?

Mystery Specks

The FBI toxicology lab examines the pills. A few tiny green specks might hold a clue.

So far, Cusack had one important piece of physical evidence: the poisoned pills. Agents carefully packed up the bottles. They shipped them to the FBI lab in Washington, D.C.

A young chemist named Roger Martz took charge of the bottles. Could he find out where the poison came from?

Martz's main job was to "fingerprint" the poison. Only three U.S. companies made cyanide. Each version had a different chemical makeup, or fingerprint. If Martz could figure out who made the cyanide, it might pinpoint where the killer bought it.

Martz examined the capsules.

He found an average of 700 mg of cyanide in each. A dose of 70 mg will kill the average adult. He also found tiny green specks in nearly all of the poisoned capsules.

Chemicals in the specks had mixed with the cyanide. That ruined Martz's attempts to fingerprint the poison. But did the specks hold an even more important clue?

Martz tested the specks. He found three chemicals normally used to kill algae in fish tanks. The killer, he decided, could have mixed the cyanide in a container used to hold the algae killer. Martz measured the exact amount of each chemical. That led him to the exact brand of algae killer.

The murderer, Martz decided, probably used a product called Algae Destroyer.

A Fish Story

The evidence piles up. Is Stella Nickell lying?

Back in Seattle, Special Agent Cusack was beginning to wonder about Stella Nickell. First of all, Nickell had not one, but two, of the poisoned bottles. The FBI had collected and tested 15,000 bottles in all. Five of them had cyanide. And Stella Nickell was unlucky enough to buy two of them? That seemed nearly impossible.

Cusack looked into Nickell's background. Just before her husband's death, the couple had been running out of money. Stella Nickell had three insurance policies on her husband's life. Two had just been bought in 1985. The third paid an extra $105,000 if Bruce Nickell died accidentally. Cyanide poisoning was an accidental death.

Police began to wonder if Stella Nickell had played a part in the poisoning death of her husband, Bruce.

Finally, Martz's test results reached Seattle. The investigator who first went to the Nickell's house remembered an important detail. Stella Nickell had a fish tank.

Cusack sent an agent to pet stores in the area with pictures of Stella Nickell. On August 25, he found a clerk who remembered her. And yes, he said, Nickell used Algae Destroyer.

Algae is the slimy green stuff that grows in fish tanks. Many fish owners use Algae Destroyer to get rid of it. Was Stella Nickell one of them?

The Final Piece

A daughter tells a tale of murder.

By the fall, Cusack thought he had found his killer. Stella Nickell came in for questioning. She said she had never bought Algae Destroyer. She also claimed she had only one insurance policy.

In December she came back to take a lie-detector test. She failed.

However, lie-detector tests cannot be used in court. So Cusack needed solid evidence. Then, in January, Nickell's 27-year-old daughter, Cindy Hamilton, called. She said her mother had talked for years about wanting to kill her husband. Stella Nickell

23

Stella Nickell had checked out two books with information about poisons. Agents found her fingerprints on one of them.

had even researched poisons at the library.

Cusack sent an agent to the local library. The FBI fingerprinting lab found 84 of Stella Nickel's prints on a book about poisons. The most handled pages were the ones on cyanide.

On December 9, 1987, Jack Cusack and Ron Nichols drove to Stella Nickell's home. They arrested her for the murder of her husband, Bruce Nickell.

In April 1988, Stella went on trial for the deaths of Sue Snow and Bruce Nickell. The prosecutor called her an "icy human being without social or moral conscience." On May 9, 1988, a **jury** found her guilty. The judge sentenced her to 99 years in jail.

All the while, Nickell has claimed she is innocent. Her daughter, Cindy, collected $250,000 in reward money from the drug companies. Nickell said Cindy lied in order to get the money. Since 1988, Stella Nickell has filed for a new trial three times. Three times her appeals have been rejected. 24/7

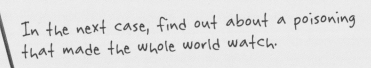

In the next case, find out about a poisoning that made the whole world watch.

The Case of the Poisoned Politician

**One night, Viktor Yushchenko
is battling for the presidency
of Ukraine. The next day, he
is fighting for his life.**

NORWEGIAN SEA

Trondheim

Bergen

EUROPE
AUSTRIA
UKRAINE
AFRICA
ASIA
RUSSIA

Ålborg   Göteborg

NORTH SEA

DENMARK
Copenhagen

Hamburg

NETHER-LANDS
Amsterdam
Düsseldorf
Köln
GERMANY
Berlin
Leipzig   Dresden
Frankfurt
LUX.

Bern
SWITZ.
Geneva

Milan
MONACO
Genoa
SAN MARINO
CORSICA (France)

Rome
VATICAN CITY
SARDINIA (Italy)
Naples
ITALY

Palermo
SICILY

Tunis

TUNISIA

26 LIBYA
Tripoli

FINLAND
Tammerfors
Helsinki

L. Onega

Viborg
L. Ladoga
St. Petersburg

Gulf of Finland
Tallinn
ESTONIA
Riga
LATVIA

RUSSIA

Nizhn Novgoro

Moscow

Smolensk

Kursk

Kaliningrad (Königsberg) (RUS.)
Gdansk (Danzig)

Vilnius
LITHUANIA

Minsk

BELARUS

Elbe R.
Vistula R.
Warsaw
Lodz
POLAND
Oder R.
Krakow
Prague
CZECH REP.
Munich
LIECHT.
Vienna
AUSTRIA
Graz
Bratislava
SLOVAKIA
Ljubljana
SLOVENIA
Budapest
HUNGARY

Kiev

UKRAINE

Kharkov

Donetsk
Ros

Dnieper R.
Dnepropetrovsk

Dniester R.
MOLDOVA
Kishinev
Odessa

Sea of Azov

CRIMEA

Venice
Po R.
Zagreb
CROATIA
SAN MARINO
BOSNIA-HERZEGOVIN
Sarajevo
MO
NE
Belgrade

ROMANIA
Bucharest

ADRIATIC SEA

Tira

Ukraine won its independence
from Russia in 1991. Ukranians
finally had the right to hold free
elections. But in the fall of 2004,
that right seemed to be in danger. A
presidential candidate said that he
had been poisoned by his opponents!

Mara

Valetta
MALTA

Nicosia
RHODES   CYPRUS
Beirut
LEBANON

CRETE

MEDITERRANEAN SEA

ISRAEL
Tel-Aviv
Jerusalem

Gulf of Sidra

EGYPT

BALTIC SEA
Volga R.
Danube R.
Rhine R.

Deadly Dinner Date

After a dinner with some political rivals, Viktor Yushchenko becomes violently ill.

On September 5, 2004, Viktor Yushchenko had an important dinner date. He hoped to become the next president of Ukraine. He was popular with the people. But his opponent had the support of the government. And in Ukraine, the government was a powerful force. It controlled the country's newspapers and TV stations. It also controlled the secret police.

The head of the secret police was hosting Yushchenko that night. They sat down to dinner at 10 P.M. with two other men. Yuschenko's bodyguards stayed behind. The men talked about Ukraine's future. They discussed Yuschenko's safety. The candidate had received death threats recently. He wanted protection from the secret police.

While they talked, the men ate crayfish and salad. They drank beer and vodka. They ended their meeting with an after-dinner drink.

At about 3:30 A.M., Yushchenko drove home. In the car, his head began to pound with pain. At home, he kissed his wife. She noticed

In 2004, Viktor Yushchenko announced that he would run for president. His main opponent was Viktor Yanukovych. Yushchenko was very popular, but Yanukovych was backed by the government.

a bitter, metallic taste on his lips. Within an hour, Yushchenko started to vomit.

Hours later, Yushchenko was rushed to the hospital. The night before, he was planning to become the next president of Ukraine. Now, he was close to death.

Written on His Face

Was Yushchenko poisoned? Or just the victim of a bad meal?

Doctors in Ukraine had no idea what was wrong with Yushchenko. They flew him to a hospital in Austria. He arrived in terrible pain. He had a crippling backache. His stomach was lined with sores. His pancreas, which creates the juices to help digest food, was swollen.

The Austrian doctors had never seen an illness like Yushchenko's. They decided the candidate's illness had been caused by chemicals not found in food.

That was all the information Yushchenko needed. He was furious. Doctors tried to keep him in the hospital. He refused. He had a campaign to run, he said. A week later, Yushchenko was back in Ukraine.

In three days, he appeared in parliament. He accused his opponents of poisoning him. "You know very well who the killer is," he said. "The killer is the government."

Yushchenko's opponents fought back. They said Yushchenko had simply had too much to drink. Others claimed he got sick from eating spoiled fish.

By this time, Yushchenko looked terrible. His face was swollen and pale. His cheeks were covered with a rash.

Many poisons can be found in the blood, and these chemicals are used to find them. After a toxicologist saw Yushchenko on TV, Yuschenko's blood was checked for poisons.

In Amsterdam, a toxicologist named Bram Brouwer saw Yushchenko on TV. He thought he recognized the rash. He wondered, Could Yushchenko have been poisoned by the deadly chemical **dioxin**?

Brouwer called the hospital in Austria. He asked for a sample of Yushchenko's blood.

Down But Not Defeated

Back from the dead, can Yushchenko win the presidency?

Yushchenko traveled his country in pain. He gave speeches and attacked his opponent. Ukraine, he said, was not yet a free country. The government was corrupt. It controlled the media. It had even tried to steal the election by murdering a candidate.

Ukranians responded with their support. Voters sent cards and letters to Yushchenko. Thousands prayed for his recovery.

But the election ended without a clear decision. It was held on October 31. Yushchenko won 39.9 percent of the vote. His opponent, Viktor Yanukovych, won 39.3 percent. The other 20 percent of voters chose minor candidates. No candidate won the 50 percent needed to make him president.

On November 21, voters went back to the polls. This time, they had to choose between Yushchenko and Yanukovych.

Yushchenko waited eagerly for the results. He was recovering but still in pain. His face still looked terribly deformed.

By December 2006, Yushchenko's face had been terribly damaged by the dioxin poisoning.

News organizations held exit polls. As Ukranians left the polling places, they were asked whom they voted for. The results showed Yushchenko in the lead. One poll said he was winning by 11 percent.

But when the vote was finally counted, the results looked much different. The official result: Yanukovych was the winner by 3 percent.

Viktor Yanukovych was Yushchenko's opponent in the 2004 election. He was declared the winner of one of the first elections.

The Orange Revolution

Ukranians march in the streets to protest the election.

After the vote, Yushchenko's supporters were furious. How could the official results be so different from the exit polls? Yushchenko insisted that the government had cheated. He refused to accept the results.

A day after the election, thousands of people filled the streets. They chanted Yushchenko's name. They waved orange flags in honor of Yushchenko's campaign color. They demanded

In December 2004, people gathered in Independence Square in Kiev to protest what they believed was an unfair election. Because Yushchenko's party used the color orange, these protests became known as the Orange Revolution.

that he be named president. Yushchenko urged them on.

As days passed, the protests grew larger. People set up tents in the streets of Kiev, the country's capital. Riot police with shields and helmets came out to meet them. Huge crowds moved to take over government buildings. The police did little to stop them.

Finally, the country's supreme court ruled the election unfair. Both sides agreed on a new election for December 26.

On December 8, protesters began to leave the streets. The "Orange Revolution" was over. Yushchenko appeared before a huge crowd. "During these 17 days, we have gotten a new country," he said.

Yushchenko turned his attention to the election. He was confident now. A new piece of news made him sure to win.

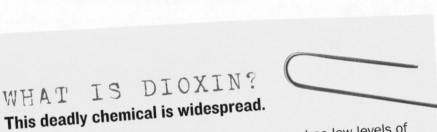

Yushchenko celebrates his victory on December 26, 2004.

On December 11, Bram Brouwer, the Dutch toxicologist, announced the results of his tests. He said that Yushchenko had been poisoned by dioxin. The level of poison in his blood was 1,000 times higher than normal.

On December 26, Yushchenko won the election with 52 percent of the vote.

WHAT IS DIOXIN?

This deadly chemical is widespread.

Don't look now! There's dioxin in your food. This deadly chemical comes from factories that use chlorine. It also comes from the manufacturing of plastics, paper, and **pesticides**.

Dioxin makes its way into the environment. It seeps into the soil. It washes into rivers. It eventually reaches animals—including you. Nearly every person has low levels of dioxin in the body.

Dioxin can be dangerous over long periods of time. It can cause cancer or birth defects. It builds up in body fat. It can stay in your body for 35 years. In the short term, high levels can cause skin rashes and digestion problems.

Case Closed?

The president takes office while the investigation continues. Was Yushchenko really poisoned?

This is the chemical makeup of dioxin.

Was Yushchenko really poisoned? A top official for Yushchenko claims the dioxin in his blood was a chemical called T-2. The Russians developed this chemical as a weapon during the Cold War. The head of Russia, Vladimir Putin, supported Yushchenko's opponent. Could the Russians have helped to poison Yushchenko?

Some people think Yushchenko was not poisoned at all. Scientists point out that dioxin doesn't act overnight. It takes several weeks for symptoms to show up. It's unlikely, then, that Yushchenko was poisoned that night at dinner. He may have been given doses of dioxin over time. But dioxin only kills over a period of years. If a killer wanted to get rid of Yushchenko, why choose dioxin?

Yushchenko still insists he was poisoned. The truth may never be known. **24/7**

This isn't the first time that poison might have been given to a politician. Find out about another unsolved toxicology mystery.

May 15, 1821
St. Helena
off the coast of Africa

The Case of the Royal Poisoning

French Emperor Napoleon Bonaparte dies after a strange illness. Can a 200-year-old lock of hair solve this historical mystery?

A History Mystery

For six years, Napoleon suffered from strange symptoms. Was someone poisoning him?

Napoleon Bonaparte spent the last six years of his life in pain. The French emperor had once ruled half of Europe. He led large armies who obeyed his commands. He challenged the governments of Italy, Egypt, and Russia. He won nearly every battle he fought.

But in 1815, Napoleon surrendered to the British army. The British sent Napoleon to an African island called St. Helena. He was to stay there for the rest of his life—which turned out to be miserable.

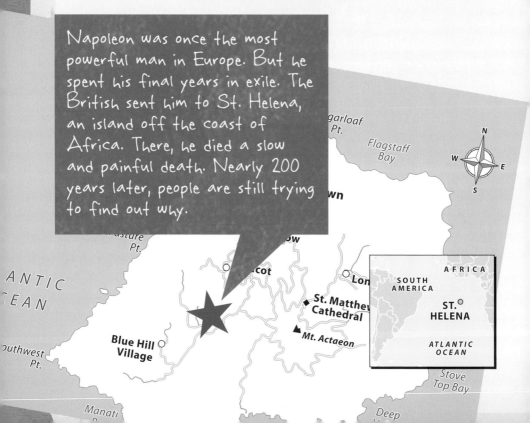

Napoleon was once the most powerful man in Europe. But he spent his final years in exile. The British sent him to St. Helena, an island off the coast of Africa. There, he died a slow and painful death. Nearly 200 years later, people are still trying to find out why.

AN EMPEROR'S LIFE
Here's a quick look at the life of Napolean Bonaparte

1769: Napoleon is born.

1796: Napoleon takes command of the French army and invades Italy.

1798: Napoleon conquers Egypt.

1799: Napoleon becomes ruler of France.

1804: Napoleon crowns himself Emperor of the French.

1805: Napoleon names himself king of Italy. He defeats the Russians and the Austrians.

1808: The French army defeats Sweden. Napoleon now controls most of Europe.

1812: Napoleon leads an army into Russia. After four months, he is forced to retreat.

1814: Napoleon's enemies invade France. Napoleon is forced to surrender. He is sent to the island of Elba.

1815: Napoleon escapes. He takes command of Paris. But in June, his army is crushed by the British. He is sent to St. Helena.

May 5, 1821: Napoleon dies after six years on St. Helena.

A painting of Napoleon from about 1803. He appears to be in good health.

Napoleon arrived in St. Helena in 1815. His health quickly started to fail. For about six years, he battled a strange illness. His legs swelled. He complained of aches and pains. He had serious headaches, diarrhea, and vomiting. He couldn't sleep.

Napoleon insisted he was being poisoned. His doctors believed he had stomach cancer or a liver problem. Finally, in May 1821, the former emperor died. His grave was dug on St. Helena. Was the truth about his death buried with his body?

Case Reopened

What really happened to Napoleon? Does modern science have the answer?

Another painting of Napoleon in healthier days. This one was painted around 1812.

During his lifetime, Napoleon failed to convince people that he was being poisoned. More than 130 years later, a Swedish dentist began to think the emperor was right.

Dr. Sten Forshufvud was a big fan of Napoleon. He loved to read about the emperor's life. In 1955, a publisher printed the **memoir** of one of Napoleon's friends. It described every terrible day of Napoleon's final month.

Forshufvud read the book with interest.

But something didn't seem right. Historians said Napoleon died of stomach cancer. But his symptoms didn't sound like cancer. Forshufvud looked up **arsenic** poisoning in a medical dictionary. Nearly all the symptoms matched Napoleon's illness.

The dentist remembered another detail. In 1840, officials decided to move Napoleon's grave to France. They dug up the emperor's body. When the casket was opened, the body looked strangely well preserved. Arsenic can have that effect.

Could it be that arsenic killed Napoleon—then kept his body from rotting? To answer that question, Forshufvud needed a piece of the emperor.

Napoleon's body at St. Helena is prepared for its return to France.

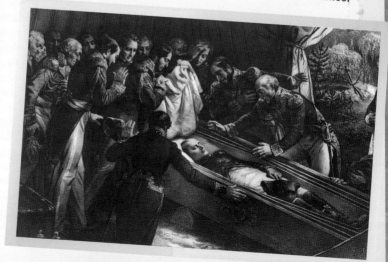

Hair-Raising Tests

How do you test for poison in a 130-year-old body?

Forshufvud knew what he had to do. He spent three years looking for samples of Napoleon's hair. He got some help from a common 19th-century tradition. The day after Napoleon died, his hair was shaved off. Friends and family members kept the locks as a way of remembering their loved one.

Forshufvud managed to buy some of the emperor's hair from collectors.

The dentist had all the evidence he needed. Now the question was: Did the hair contain traces of arsenic? If so, how much? And when did the poison enter Emperor Napoleon's body?

Forshufvud sent the strands to Dr. Hamilton Smith in England. Smith had developed a way to measure toxins in hair.

Smith's method involves splitting the hair sample into tiny particles. The particles can then be analyzed using a device called a **spectrometer**.

Smith's spectrometer showed exactly what Forshfvud expected. Napoleon had a high level of arsenic in his body.

Smith and Forshfvud weren't done yet.

They wanted to know exactly when the levels of arsenic in Napoleon's body rose. They figured that hair grows an inch (2.5 cm) every two months. The strands in their sample were three inches long. These hairs represented the last six months of Napoleon's life.

The scientists divided the hair into sections. They measured the arsenic in each section. They found that during some weeks Napoleon took in large amounts of arsenic. During other weeks, the amounts were much smaller.

Now they compared their results to the memoir. Did Napoleon's health in the final weeks of his life match the arsenic levels? The two timelines matched perfectly. Napoleon had been miserable when arsenic levels were high. His health improved when the levels were low.

Smith and Forshufvud were ready to make their conclusion. In 1961, they published their findings. Napoleon, they said, had been murdered.

POISON ALERT
What is arsenic, and what does it do to the body?

There's arsenic in your body right now. How'd it get there? Arsenic is a metal. It can be found in rocks, soil, even the air. Drinking water often contains small amounts of the poison.

Arsenic is also added to many products. It helps keep building materials—like wood—from rotting. It's used in some paints, dyes, drugs, and soaps. It's also added to pesticides and weed killers.

Everyone is exposed to low levels of arsenic. For most people, that's not a problem. In high doses, however, arsenic can be very dangerous. It can cause cancer or skin disease. It can also damage the liver and kidneys.

Killer Wallpaper?

Could it be the murderer wasn't a person at all?

A lot of people were not convinced that Napoleon had been poisoned. But Ben Weider became a true believer. Weider is a millionaire businessman from Canada. He is also extremely interested in Napoleon.

After Forshufvud announced his results, Weider spent the next four decades researching Napoleon. He read everything he could find about the emperor. He searched far and wide for more hair samples. When he found them, he paid for new tests.

In 1995, Weider had the FBI test new hair samples. In 2001, he sent five more strands to a French team. Both tests found high levels of poison in the samples. The French team said Napoleon had seven to 38 times more arsenic in him than is normal.

But did the poison really come from a murderer?

Some people think Napoleon took in the arsenic little by little during his daily life. In the 1880s, many products were made with arsenic. Shampoos and other hair products had arsenic in them. Some medicines contained small amounts of the poison. Some colored dyes were made with arsenic.

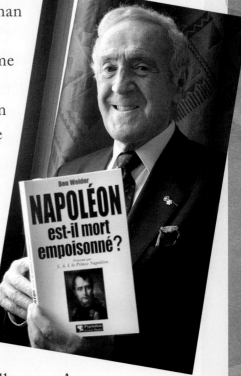

Ben Weider is president of the International Napoleonic Society. He is holding his book, *Was Napoleon Poisoned?*

According to one theory, Napoleon was killed by his wallpaper. A series of strange deaths in the 1800s puzzled doctors. In 1893, the deaths were traced to a

The green dye in Napoleon's wallpaper had high levels of arsenic in it. Could that have killed him? This paper was taken from one of the rooms in Napoleon's house on St. Helena. You can see the green dye outlining the designs.

green dye used in wallpaper. The dye had high levels of arsenic in it. In damp rooms, it formed a mold that was highly toxic.

On St. Helena, Napoleon often took long, steamy baths to relax. What was one of the colors in his bathroom wallpaper? Green.

Was one of the most powerful men in history killed by his wallpaper? Or did someone poison him slowly and secretly? No one knows for sure.

Some people still insist that stomach cancer was the real killer. They say there's no way to prove that the hair samples Ben Weider used came from Napoleon.

Weider wants to dig up the emperor's body to make sure. Until then, the truth will probably stay buried. 24/7

FORENSIC DOWNLOAD

Here's even more amazing stuff about forensic toxicology for you to swallow.

IN THIS SECTION:

▶ why people used to take arsenic to make them FEEL BETTER;

▶ why FORENSIC TOXICOLOGY is making headlines;

▶ the TOOLS that are used to study toxins;

▶ whether forensic toxicology might be in YOUR FUTURE?

1

400s B.C. **A Deadly Cure**
The Greek doctor Hippocrates *(left)* used arsenic to treat stomach problems. That's pretty weird when you realize that he was also famous for his motto, which is now called the Hippocratic Oath. That motto includes the promise to "Do no harm."

Key Dates in Forensic

1850 **Detecting Poison**
French scientist Jean Servois Stas invented a way to find poison in a victim's body. A victim had died of chemical burns in his mouth. Stas poured **ether**, a type of alcohol, on the victim's tissues. The ether evaporated and the drug was left behind. It was **nicotine**, the chemical used in cigarettes. Stas helped prove that the killer forced the victim to eat tobacco.

1906 **Color Coded**
Russian plant scientist Alexandr Tswett found a new way to identify chemicals. It's called paper **chromatography**. The process separates small amounts of substances from one another. Each substance creates a different colored band on paper. Scientists study that band to learn about the substance. Today, toxicologists use a similar method to test for chemicals.

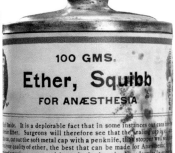

100 GMS.
Ether, Squibb
FOR ANÆSTHESIA

It is a deplorable fact that in some instances out can he... Ether. Surgeons will therefore see that the sealing cap is the... cut out the soft metal cap with a penknife, than stopper well... the quality of ether, the best that can be made for Anæsthesia... not only as a general Anæsthetic, but also hypodermically or... and as a Reagent. Average D... **Antidotes:** *artificial respiration with in...*

399 B.C. First Famous Poisoning

Greek rulers sentenced the philosopher Socrates to death by poisoning. The charge? Corrupting the minds of young people. Socrates (above, center) was given a drink made with the deadly poison **hemlock**.

1752 Science in Court

An English court sentenced Mary Blandy (below) to death by hanging for poisoning her father. She had wanted to marry a Scottish captain—against her father's wishes. The captain sent Mary a powder, which she spread on her father's food. At the trial, scientists testified that the powder was arsenic. Their evidence? It looked and smelled like arsenic. Blandy's trial was the first to use toxicology as evidence.

Toxicology

Poisons have been used to kill since ancient times. Check out this timeline about the world's poisonous past.

2004 Poisoned Politician?

Ukranian presidential candidate Viktor Yushchenko claimed he was poisoned by his opponents. He went on to win the election.

1950s Toxicology Takes Off

Forensic toxicologists got new high-tech tools. Ultraviolet lights, x-rays, and gas chromatographs helped them track down hard-to-find poisons.

Name Your Poison

Have a look at some of the equipment and forms used by forensic toxicologists. And find out what to do if you suspect a child has been poisoned.

EQUIPMENT

Say toxicologists suspect that someone has drugs in his or her system. There are countless possibilities. To figure out which drug it is, toxicologists often have to do at least two levels of tests: screening and confirming.

Screening tests show that some kind of drug or toxin is mostly likely present.

Confirming tests are more sensitive and can confirm the presence of a poison.

Here's a look at some of these tests.

SCREENING

IMMUNOSSAY TEST

This test can **detect** certain kinds of drugs in the body. **Immunoassay** of urine samples can detect aspirin. It can also detect barbiturates, a kind of drug that calms people down and can even put them to sleep. And it can detect cocaine and other narcotic drugs.

THIN-LAYER CHROMATOGRAPH

This test can separate out all the various parts of a chemical. It can test for hundreds of different substances at once.

CONFIRMING

GAS CHROMATOGRAPH WITH MASS SPECTROMETRY

The gas chromatograph can separate the sample into all its chemical parts. The mass spectrometry can then identify all these parts.

POISONING FACT SHEET

What should I do if I think a child has been poisoned?

Call your local poison center right away. Do not wait for the child to look or feel sick! Follow these first-aid steps:

■ Swallowed Poisons

- Do not give the victim anything to eat or drink before calling the poison center or a doctor.
- Do not make the child throw up or give ipecac syrup unless a doctor or the poison center tells you to.

■ Inhaled Poisons

- Get the victim to fresh air right away. Call the poison center.

■ Poisons on the Skin

- Remove contaminated clothing and rinse the child's skin with water for 10 minutes. Call the poison center.

■ Poisons in the Eye

- Flush the child's eye for 15 minutes using a large cup filled with lukewarm water held 2–4 inches (5–10 cm) from the eye. Call the poison center.

For more poison prevention and first aid information or to locate your local poison center, visit the American Association of Poison Control Centers Web site at: www.aapcc.org

This sheet is made available through the financial support of Health Resources and Services Administration Maternal Child Health Bureau.

Drug Analysis Request Form

Boxes 1 Through 6 MUST BE COMPLETED

(1) Type of Case (Check Proper Box in Each Column)

Type of Case
- ☐ Fatal Accident
- ☐ P.I. Accident
- ☐ P.D. Accident
- ☐ Homicide
- ☐ OWI
- ☐ Suicide
- ☐ Other (Specify)_____

Status of Subject
- ☐ Dead
- ☐ Injured
- ☐ Not Injured

Inv_____

Medical examiners or police officers fill out forms like this one. Such forms tell toxicologists exactly what to look for.

(2) Subject Information

Name of Subject (Last, First, Mid_____tial)

Street Address

The victim's name and other information goes here.

☐ Female

(3) Submitting Agency

Inves_____ing Officer/Coroner

Agency

Investigators, police officers, or medical examiners put their information here. It tells toxicologists who is requesting the testing.

____cy Case #

____y of Occurrence

ORI #

(4) Collection Data and Chain of Custody Information

Specimen Taken By:_____

Date Taken: _____   Time Taken: _____

Loca_____
am W
pm

Received From   Released To

Received From   Released To

Received From   Released To

Received From   Released To

This section is important—especially in court. The chain of custody tracks who handled the evidence and when. It starts when an officer or a medical examiner finds a sample. After that, every time evidence changes hands, it must be recorded. The fewer people in the chain of custody, the better. Every time people handle a piece of evidence, they can damage it.

This section tells toxicologists if the victim was given a breath test for alcohol.

(5) Breath Test

Was a valid chemical breath test administered by a certified operator as defined in PL 143-1983 and ICS 11-4-5?   ☐ Yes   ☐ No

The investigators who order the toxicology test decide what drugs to test for. They also check off the type of sample: blood, urine, or other (such as tissues or organs).

(6) Drug Requests

Drug Panel	Drugs
Alcohol	Ethanol
Drug Screen I	Barbiturates, Benzodiazepines, Cannabinoids, Cocaine, and Opiates
Drug Screen II	Screen I + Amphetamines, Methadone, Phencyclidine, and Propoxyphene
Single Class Drug Screen	Specify (Drug Classes Listed Above) _____ ☐ Blood ☐ Urine
Other Drug Requests	Specify _____ _____

All Positive blood ethanol results will ~ other drug classes, confirmatory ~ the presence and to quantif~ ~ or s~

This section gives investigators step-by-step instructions on how to handle evidence and samples. It also explains how to take samples from a victim.

(7) Instructions

Instructions to Investigating Officer:
1. Fill out the Drug Analysis Request Form completely and legibly.
2. Witness the collection of the samples.
   A. Blood should be collected in the gray stoppered tubes.
   B. Urine should be collected in the specimen bottle.
3. Fill out all information requested on the blood tube label(s) and/or urine bottle label.
4. Return filled blood tubes to the styrofoam holder.
5. Place styrofoam ~ ~ ~ in the ziploc bag.

DO N~

6. Affix evidence ~
7. Place complet~
8. Reassemble k~
9. Send specime~

Instructions to Physician or ~
1. Clean skin wi~
2. Draw blood v~
3. If drawing bl~
4. To ensure p~
   (Do Not Sha~
5. "Location" r~

American Board of Forensic Toxicology Guidelines

6.4 Recommended Amounts of Specimens

Many deaths involve ingestion of multiple drugs, necessitating larger amounts of tissue and fluids to be collected at autopsy for toxicological examination. The following is a suggested list of specimens and amounts to be collected at autopsy in such cases:

Brain: 50 gm
Liver: 50 gm
Kidney: 50 gm
Heart blood: 25 ml
Peripheral blood: 10 ml
Vitreous humor: all available
Bile: all available
Urine: all available
Gastric contents: all available

HELP WANTED:
Forensic Toxicologist

Can you picture yourself as a forensic toxicologist? Here's more information about the field.

David Vidal is a senior criminalist for the Los Angeles County Sheriff's Department in California.

Q&A: DR. DAVID VIDAL

24/7: Why did you decide to become a forensic toxicologist?

VIDAL: I started out in a hospital lab, which is very different from a crime lab. I jumped into forensic toxicology because it's a more interesting and exciting job.

24/7: What's the best part about your job?

VIDAL: The lab work. I like analyzing things and working on machines. It's nice when we get unexpected results.

24/7: Can you solve a case in one hour, like they do on crime scene shows?

VIDAL: Not really. But some of the cases that we've worked on in our lab show up on *CSI*. Some of our retired lab people work with the show.

24/7: What kind of cases do you normally work on?

VIDAL: We usually test for drugs in blood and urine. But sometimes we get poisoning cases. They might involve food-tampering or poison in liquids. Another case might be pet poisoning, where someone stuffs pills into a raw hamburger and throws it over the fence for the neighbor's dog. Another case might involve testing vomit for a dangerous club drug.

24/7: What's the hardest part?

VIDAL: Most people would probably say testifying in court. It's a lot of pressure. You have to be tough-minded and thick-skinned. But the work that we do is important for society, for court, for victims of a crime, and for the accused.

24/7: What's your advice for people who are thinking about a career in forensic toxicology?

VIDAL: [Work hard in] high school and college. You'll need a degree in a hard science, such as chemistry, biology, biochemistry, or microbiology. Besides studying hard, it's a good idea to get involved and do volunteer work at a crime lab. You'll get to learn about the real world inside a crime lab.

THE STATS

DAY JOB: Most forensic toxicologists work in crime labs for city, county, or state governments. The FBI and other federal agencies have their own forensic toxicology labs. Forensic toxicologists can also work for hospitals and sports agencies that test for drugs and steroids in athletes.

MONEY: $45,000–$100,000

EDUCATION: Forensic toxicologists must finish the following:
▶ 4 years of college
▶ graduate school to receive a master's or doctoral degree
▶ certification by the American Board of Forensic Toxicology

THE NUMBERS: The international association of forensic toxicologists has 1400 members worldwide.

Take this totally unscientific quiz to find out if forensic toxicology might be a good career for you.

1 **Toxicologists work with chemicals and dead bodies—which can have strong smells. How do you feel about sniffing odors all day?**

a) No problem. That's what noses are for!

b) I prefer to smell flowers, but I can put up with nasty scents.

c) Gross! Take me to the nearest perfume counter!

2 **As a forensic toxicologist, you'll be handling blood, urine, and body tissues. Would you mind that?**

a) Bring me those latex gloves! I can't wait to test this stuff in a lab.

b) I'm a bit freaked out by blood, but I might be able to handle it.

c) Keep that away from me!

3 **How are you with following directions?**

a) I follow directions step-by-step and check my work.

b) I try to follow directions most of the time, but sometimes I might skip a step.

c) I don't like following directions. I prefer to wing it.

4 **When I want to learn more about something, I:**

a) ask questions, search the Internet, read books about it.

b) ask my friends.

c) go back to sleep.

5 **How do you feel about speaking in front of a group of people?**

a) I'm comfortable making a presentation in front of a crowd.

b) I'm a bit shy and not very confident when people focus on me.

c) I try to avoid it as much as possible.

YOUR SCORE

Give yourself 3 points for every "**a**" you chose. Give yourself 2 points for every "**b**" you chose. Give yourself 1 point for every "**c**" you chose.

If you got **13–15 points**, you'd probably be a good forensic toxicologist.

If you got **10–12 points**, you might be a good forensic toxicologist.

If you got **5–9 points**, you might want to look at another career!

HOW TO GET STARTED...NOW!

It's never too early to start working toward your goals.

GET AN EDUCATION

▶ Focus on your science classes, such as chemistry and biology.

▶ Start thinking about college. Look for ones with good biochemistry and pharmacology programs.

▶ Read the newspaper. Keep up with what's going on in your community.

▶ Read anything you can find about forensic toxicology. See the books and Web sites in the Resources section on pages 56–58.

▶ Graduate from high school!

NETWORK!

▶ Find out about forensic groups in your area.

▶ See if you can find a local toxicologist who might be willing to give you advice. Or look for someone on the Web.

GET AN INTERNSHIP

▶ Look for an internship with a toxicologist.

▶ Look for an internship in a local forensic lab.

LEARN ABOUT OTHER JOBS IN THE FIELD

▶ criminalist

▶ biochemist

▶ forensic biologist

Resources

Looking for more information about forensic toxicology? Here are some resources you don't want to miss!

PROFESSIONAL ORGANIZATIONS

American Academy of Forensic Sciences (AAFS)
www.aafs.org
410 North 21st Street
Colorado Springs, CO 80904-2798
PHONE: 719-636-1100
FAX: 719-636-1993

The AAFS is a professional society dedicated to the application of science to the law. It promotes education and accuracy in the forensic sciences.

Forensic Toxicologist Certification Board, Inc.
http://home.usit.net/~robsears/
ftcb/index.htm
P.O. Box 21398
Columbia, SC 29221-1398
PHONE: 803-896-7365
FAX: 803-896-7542

The Forensic Toxicologist Certification Board was established in 1992.

International Association of Forensic Toxicologists
www.tiaft.org
211 East Chicago Ave.
Chicago, IL 60611-2678
PHONE: 312-440-2500

The International Association of Forensic Toxicologists is 45 years old. It works to promote cooperation among members and to encourage research in forensic toxicology.

Society of Forensic Toxicologists, Inc. (SOFT)
www.soft-tox.org
P.O. Box 5543
Mesa, AZ 85211-5543
PHONE/FAX: 480-839-9106

SOFT is an organization made up of practicing forensic toxicologists who are interested in promoting and developing forensic toxicology.

WEB SITES

American Board of Forensic Toxicology
www.abft.org
This Web site offers information and links for toxicologists. Offers lab accreditation.

California Association of Toxicologists
www.cal-tox.org
This Web site includes space for members to communicate and recent publications on the study of toxicology.

The Evidence: A Forensic Science Technology Journal
www.theevidence.ca/
This is a Web site that publishes research being done in toxicology and other forensic sciences.

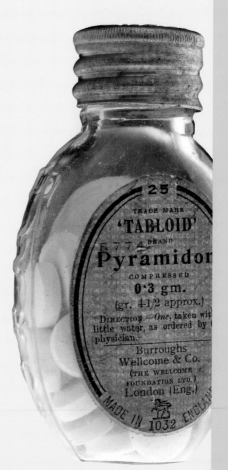

BOOKS ABOUT FORENSIC SCIENCE AND TOXICOLOGY

Emsley, John. *The Elements of Murder: A History of Poison.* New York: Oxford University Press, 2005.

Evans, Colin. *The Casebook of Forensic Detection: How Science Solved 100 of the World's Most Baffling Crimes.* Indianapolis: Wiley, 1999.

James, Stuart, and Jon J. Nordby. *Forensic Science: An Introduction to Scientific and Investigative Techniques, 2nd ed.* Boca Raton, Fla.: CRC Books, 2005.

Macinnis, Peter. *Poisons: From Hemlock to Botox to the Killer Bean of Calabar.* New York: Arcade Publishing, 2005.

Smith, Fred. *Handbook of Forensic Drug Analysis.* Burlington, Mass.: Academic Press, 2004.

Trestrail, John Harris. *Criminal Poisoning: Investigational Guide for Law Enforcement, Toxicologists, Forensic Scientists, and Attorneys.* Totowa, N.J.: Humana Press, 2000.

Turkington, Carol. *The Poisons and Antidotes Sourcebook, 2nd ed.* New York: Checkmark Books, 1999.

BOOKS ABOUT FORENSIC SCIENCE FOR KIDS

Innes, Brian. *The Search for Forensic Evidence.* Milwaukee: Gareth Stevens Publishing, 2005.

Platt, Richard. *Forensics.* Boston: Kingfisher, 2005.

Rainis, Kenneth G. *Crime-Solving Science Projects: Forensic Science Experiments.* Berkeley Heights, N.J.: Enslow Publishing, 2000.

Walker, Pam, and Elaine Wood. *Crime Scene Investigations: Real-Life Science Labs for Grades 6–12.* New York: Jossey-Bass, 1998.

A

acute (uh-KYOOT) *adjective* describing something that is quick and intense. An acute poisoning is serious and happens very fast.

arsenic (AHR-suh-nik) *noun* a metallic poison found in wood preservatives and other products

autopsy (AW-top-see) *noun* an examination of a body to determine how and why a person died

B

bile (byle) *noun* a liquid produced by the liver that can show what toxins are in someone's body

C

chain of custody (chayn uhv KUH-stuh-dee) *noun* a list of people who handle evidence. The fewer people who handle the samples, the better. In court, lawyers can attack toxicology tests if sample evidence is not handled properly.

chemical (KEM-i-cull) *noun* a human-made substance created from two or more materials

chromatography (kro-muh-TAH-graff-ee) *noun* a laboratory test that separates every material in a substance or chemical

chronic (KRAH-nik) *adjective* describing something that happens over time. A chronic poisoning occurs gradually and in small doses.

coma (KOH-muh) *noun* a state of deep sleep (unconsciousness) caused by disease or illness

conscious (KON-shush) *adjective* awake or aware of what is going on. An unconscious person is alive but cannot hear or see anything.

cyanide (SYe-uh-nyde) *noun* a fatal poison that is found in dyes, insect killers, and other products

D

detect (di-TEKT) *verb* to notice or discover something

dioxin (DYE-ohk-sun) *noun* a deadly chemical that is used in the manufacture of plastics, paper, and pesticides

drug (druhg) *noun* a natural product or human-made chemical that can change the way the body works

E

ether (EE-thur) *noun* a type of alcohol often used to help dissolve other materials

evidence (EHV-uh-denss) *noun* things that help prove someone is guilty or innocent

expert (EX-purt) *noun* someone who knows a lot about a subject. See page 12 for a list of forensic experts.

F

FBI (EF-bee-eye) *noun* a part of the U.S. government that investigates major crimes. It stands for *Federal Bureau of Investigation*.

forensic (fuh-REN-zik) *adjective* relating to a kind of science used to help investigate crimes

H

hemlock (HEM-lok) *noun* a poisonous plant or a deadly drink made from that plant

I

immunoassay (IH-myoo-noh-ah-SAY) *noun* a test that detects if certain substances are in a person's body and, if so, how much there is

J

jury (JUR-ee) *noun* a group of people who listen to a court case and decide if someone is guilty or innocent

M

ME (EM-ee) *noun* a medical doctor who investigates suspicious deaths. It is short for *medical examiner*.

memoir (MEM-whar) *noun* a book that a person writes about his or her own life

N

nicotine (NIK-uh-teen) *noun* a poisonous substance found in tobacco

P

pesticide (PEST-uh-side) *noun* a chemical that kills insects

poison (POY-zuhn) *verb* to give someone any substance that causes injury, illness, or death

S

spectometer (spek-TOM-uh-tur) *noun* a device used to study tiny particles

symptom (SIMP-tum) *noun* a sign of illness or some physical problem

T

toxic (TOK-sik) *adjective* poisonous

toxicology (TOK-sik-ahl-uh-jee) *noun* the science of finding, treating, or studying poisons, drugs, and chemicals

toxin (TOK-sihn) *noun* any substance that can kill cells or cause injury or death. A poison.

V

victim (VIK-tuhm) *noun* a person who has been hurt, mistreated, or killed

Index

Author's Note

Writing this book has turned me into a scientific sleuth. It's difficult to track down information regarding poisoning cases. Because most poisoning cases involve a victim, a murderer, or court, getting people to discuss a case is tough work.

Luckily, there's lots of information on the Internet, in toxicology journals, and in books. And toxicologists are more than happy to share information about their scientific field—as long as you don't show their names or faces in the book!

The majority of toxicologists work for city, county, or state-run crime labs. Because these toxicologists testify in court, their credibility might be compromised if their names, photos, and other information are splashed across a book. To avoid this problem, I've had to use anonymous helpers to gather information.

ACKNOWLEDGMENTS

I would like to thank Barry A.J. Fisher and David Vidal (top-secret state toxicologist) for taking the time to talk about their work.

CONTENT ADVISER: Christopher Long, PhD, DABFT, Director of St. Louis University Forensic and Environmental Toxicology Laboratories